DEW DROPS

朝露

DRBA/BTTS/DRBU

Dew Drops 朝露 : Pearls of Wisdom by the Venerable Master Hua
Illustrated by: O.M.

Published and translated by:
    Buddhist Text Translation Society
    1777 Murchison Drive
    Burlingame, CA 94010-4504
    www.drba.org

© 2003 Buddhist Text Translation Society
    Dharma Realm Buddhist University
    Dharma Realm Buddhist Association

Second printing, 2007

11 10 09 08   10 9 8 7 6 5 4 3 2

Printed in Taiwan

    Library of Congress Cataloging-in-Publication Data

Hsuan Hua, 1908-
    Dew drops : pearls of wisdom by the Venerable Master Hua =
        [Zhao lu : Xuanhuashangren yi li ming zhu]
    p. cm.
English and Chinese
ISBN 978-088139-862-5
1. Buddhism--Juvenile literature. 2. Conduct of life--Juvenile
literature. I. Title: Zhao lu. II. Title.

BQ4032.H76 2003
294.3'4432--dc21
                        2003056258

DEW DROPS

獻給您——衣裏明珠莫外尋

Dedicated to you—
The Pearl of Wisdom
is within ourselves,
and we should not seek
for it from the outside.

Our idle thoughts are like waves
Created as winds blow across the ocean.
If you calm the winds of bad karma,
Your idle thoughts will diminish.
How do you calm these winds?
Simply avoid creating bad karma.
Abandon all evil deeds
and perform wholesome ones.

妄想好像大海，一旦風起，則興起波浪。
波浪是從風那裏來的，
所以把業風平靜，妄想便少了。
怎樣平業風？

就是不造惡業。
所謂「諸惡莫作，眾善奉行。」

One good thought
can bring peace to the world.

One evil thought
can cause terrible storms and gales.

一念善，天地間就吉祥：
一念惡，天地間就有狂風暴雨。

Take heed! Take heed!

Always finish whatever you begin.
Do not allow adverse circumstances
To deter you from realizing your vows.

切記！切記！

無論做什麼事，要有始有終，
不要為外境搖動，而退失自己的志願。

Whatever little bit you know,
You should put into practice.
Little by little, it will accumulate,
Just as tiny grains
of sand can form a stupa.
In time you will ultimately succeed.

我們要知道一點，就去行一點，
積少成多，集沙成塔，功到自然成。

A cultivator of the Way
Must not covet anything,
whether good or bad.
The Way exists in an ordinary state of mind.
Behave normally without being greedy.
Being greedy is a mistake.

人修道，無論什麼也不要貪，
好的也不貪，壞的也不貪，
平常心是道。
要平平常常的，不要生一種貪心，
你貪什麼都是不對的。

Little children are like young trees.
While they are growing up,
they need to be pruned,
So they can become pillars of society.

小孩子如小樹枝般長大，
枝椏七八，
必須砍去橫枝，
將來才會成為棟樑之材。

Everything in the world,
whether positive or negative,
Is a lesson of awakening for us.
Positive things make us awaken
to what's positive.
Negative things inspire us
to awaken to adversity.

這世界上無論好和不好，都是教人覺悟。
好，就是教你覺悟好的地方；
不好，就是教你覺悟不好的地方。

Patience is a priceless jewel
That no one knows how to use.
If everyone could utilize it,
All would be well.

忍是無價寶，人人使不好，
若能會用它，萬事都能了。

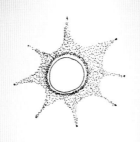

16

Cultivating means being at peace,
Free from afflictions and arrogance.

修行是平平靜靜，
無煩惱、無貢高我慢。

Cultivators must return to the zero.
We must go back to our original source.
Our nature's brilliant treasury is full
and perfect--The wisdom
of the perfect mirror has no deficiency.

修道人要恢復到○，
返本還原，
圓滿自性的大光明藏，
大圓鏡智，什麼也不缺。

Lessen your desires and be content
with what you have.
Then, nothing at all can trouble you.

少欲知足，就沒有一切的麻煩了。

22

The great sages and eminent monks of old
Always came and went without leaving a trace.
They drifted in and then floated away,
Coming and going without a care or worry.
It is as if they had never come or gone.

古來的大德高僧，
往往都是來無影，去無蹤，
來也飄飄，去也飄飄，
來也無罣無礙，去也無罣無礙，
不如不來也不去。

The Way is realized
through singleness of mind,
Just as an army is valued for its skill,
not its size.

Be mindful in every move and action.
Watch what you say when living with others.
Guard against the thieves of the eyes,
Ears, nose, tongue, body, and mind.
Do not be swayed by these six thieves.

道在專一，兵在精不在多。

我們一舉一動，不離自心，
群居守口，
防眼、耳、鼻、舌、身、意六賊，
不被六賊所轉。

Cultivators must develop patience.
You must be able to endure heat,
cold, wind, and rain.
Be able to bear hunger, thirst, scoldings,
and beatings.

修行人，就要修忍的功夫。
忍熱忍寒，忍風忍雨，
忍飢忍渴，忍罵忍打。

Virtue can be compared
to the sun and moon,
heaven and earth, and to one's very life.
Being without virtue is
like being without life itself,
as well as being without the sun and moon,
And without heaven and earth.

道德就等於日月，
也等於天地，也等於人的性命。
沒有道德，
就等於人沒有性命，沒有日月天地一樣。

The Buddhadharma
is as deep as a great ocean.
You must practice with diligence
With vigor you can achieve your aims.

佛法深如大海，
必須勇猛精進，勤加修習，
才能有所成就。

Perfecting the study
of Buddhism means learning
To be compassionate and virtuous
And to forgive others instead of arguing
Or fighting with them.

學佛要學慈悲、道德、原諒人；
不和人起對待，不和人起鬥爭。

True happiness comes
when you seek nothing.

When you seek nothing,
you have no worries.

真正的快樂，是無求的，
「到無求處便無憂」。

What is a mountain?
It is our arrogance.
What is an ocean?
It is our sense of inferiority.

If you are arrogant,
then there are high mountains.
If you feel inferior,
then there is a vast ocean.

什麼叫山？就是我們的貢高心。
什麼叫海？就是我們的自卑感。

你有貢高心，就是有高山。
你有自卑感，就是有大海。

If people do not realize Buddhahood,
It is because they merely talk
and do not practice.

人不成佛，
就是因為儘在口頭禪上用功夫。

Not to seek,
not to be greedy,
not to be selfish,
Not to contend,
not to pursue personal advantage,
And not to lie are the most effective ways
to cultivate.

不爭、不貪、不求、
不自私、不自利、不打妄想，
這是最有效的

修行方法。

W hat are idle thoughts?
They are just the churning of our desires.

什麼是妄想？
妄想就是欲念紛飛。

All things
and creatures are turning the Dharma wheel.
Humans turn the Dharma wheel of humans.
Squirrels turn the Dharma wheel of squirrels.
If you understand,
you have heard the Dharma of understanding.
If you don't understand,
you have heard the Dharma of ignorance.

萬事萬物都在轉法輪，
人在轉人的法輪，松鼠在轉松鼠的法輪。
你若明白了，就聽到明白的法；
若不明白，就聽到愚癡的法。

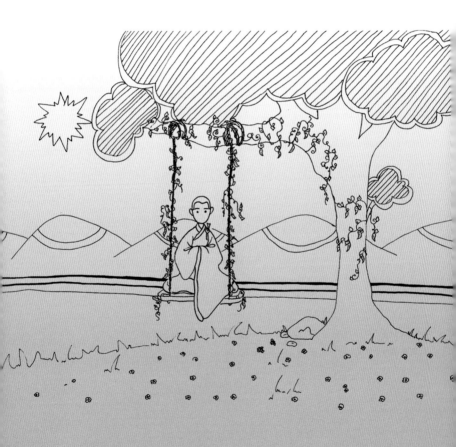

You insist on being lazy
Despite the peril of birth and death!
If you pay no heed
and act as if you don't care,
Then you are truly wasting your time!

生死那麼危險，還要懶惰！
若無其事，好像自己有定力，豈不是空過光陰！

When a man's dog or chicken runs away,
he will search for it,
Yet when his mind wanders off,
It does not occur to him to look for his mind.
People seek after petty things
and forget what is important.

人養狗、養雞，若牠們跑到外面去，
人都會各處找雞、找狗。
可是心跑了，就不知去找，
捨本逐末，把根本忘了，撿起末梢。

A cultivator who fears solitude
Will not be able to cultivate.

修行人若怕孤獨，
那就不能修行。

In cultivation,
obstacles cannot be eliminated by force.
If you are sincere,
obstacles will melt away of themselves.

修道時不用強力去對抗障礙，
如果你真誠，
障礙會自然地冰消瓦解。

54

When you are no longer greedy,
You will be able to let go.
When you can let go, you will be at peace.
When you are at peace, you will realize
Great wisdom and enlightenment.

你沒有貪心了，才能放下。
放下，才能得到自在。
你能得到自在，
然後才能開大智慧，大開圓覺。

The sea of suffering is boundless;
Yet a turn of the head is the other shore.
Don't keep drifting in this sea
Or else you will never escape.

所謂「苦海無邊，回頭是岸。」
不要在苦海中漂浮沉沒了，
否則將無解脫出離之日。

Cultivators must dispel idle thoughts,
Emotions, and desires.
They must sweep them all out
And clean up their minds.

我們修道一定要把七情六欲之妄想，
大掃除一番，清理得乾乾淨淨。

Affliction sets your mind on fire.
Free from afflictions,
you are clear and refreshed.
Who told you to get afflicted?

你若煩惱，就是熱惱：
你不煩惱，就是清涼。

誰叫你生煩惱的？

When you cultivate, don't wear a mask.
Don't advertise one thing and sell another.
Avoid doing anything that's against the law.
To cultivate,
you must be genuine and down-to-earth.
Actually do the work yourself.

修行不能戴假面具，
掛羊頭賣狗肉，做一些不合法的事。
修行要真真實實，腳踏實地，躬行實踐。

64

Don't look for trouble,
And don't be afraid of trouble.

不找麻煩，不怕麻煩。

If you set aside your own body and mind,
Then you will become a Buddha.

放下身心佛自成。

In cultivation,
we must stay balanced, like a scale.
How do we stay balanced?
The key is to always be tranquil.
There should be no waves in our inherent nature.

修行要天天保持像個秤似的，
平衡下來。
怎麼平衡下來呢？
就是時時刻刻都要平平靜靜的，
自性一點波浪也沒有。

The happiness of the Saha world is ephemeral.
The ultimate bliss of cultivation is everlasting.
That's why we must cultivate.

世界的快樂是短暫的，
究竟的快樂是永遠的，
所以才要修道。

You must be a dragon or elephant for Buddhism, not a mouse.

要做法門的龍象，
不要做法門的老鼠。

If you understand,
everything will reflect
The intent of the Patriarch from the West.
If you don't understand,
Your temper will flare in every situation.

你若懂了，事事都是「西來祖師意」；
你若不懂，「樣樣都生氣」。

Compassion comes from
within your own nature.
It is not the least bit contrived or artificial.
Deliberately trying
to please others is nothing but hypocrisy.

慈悲源於自性，無須半點矯揉造作，
不是故意去討好人，
這就落於虛偽。

Set aside your petty cleverness
and smartness.
Don't think that you understand
and know everything.
If you think you know everything,
Then you don't really understand Buddhism.

要把你那些小聰明、小智慧都收起來，
不要覺得自己什麼都明白，什麼都懂。
如果你覺得自己什麼都明白，
那就是沒有真正明白佛法。

When we cultivate,
The most important thing
is to avoid contention.
Not contending means
not arguing with anyone
About rights and wrongs.

我們修道時，

最重要的是不爭：

不爭是不和任何人爭長論短，

爭是爭非。

82

If you want to avert calamities,
You must investigate
the true principles of life.
Once you understand these true principles,
You will know
where these calamities come from.

想要消滅種種的災難，
必須要研究人生的真理：
把人生的真理明白了，
才能知道這些災難的來源。

One day of not losing your temper
Is one day of cultivation.
Ten days of not losing your temper
Is ten days of cultivation.
If you lose your temper,
Then you have no cultivation.

一天不發脾氣，就是一天的修行，

十天不發脾氣，就是十天的修行；

若發脾氣，就是沒有修行。

In cultivating the Way,
you must cultivate true virtue.
Do not hinder others,
and do not be afraid if they hinder you.

修道就是要修真正的道德，
不妨礙他人，也不怕他人妨礙自己。

As cultivators,
we must bring forth from our hearts
Genuine, great, and powerful vows,
And then we must put these vows
into practice.

我們修道的人，
都應該要發真正的
從內心發出來的大願大力，
然後照著這個願力去實行。

法界佛教總會簡介

· 創辦人宣化上人。

· 以法界為體，將佛教的真實義理，

　傳播到世界各地為目的；

　以翻譯經典、弘揚正法、

　提倡道德教育、利樂一切有情為己任。

‧以不爭、不貪、不求、不自私、不自利、不妄語為宗旨。

‧有萬佛聖城等近三十座道場,遍佈美、亞洲;
　其僧眾均須恪遵佛制:日中一食、衣不離體,
　持戒念佛,習教參禪,和合共住,獻身佛教。

‧有國際譯經學院、法界宗教研究院、僧伽居士訓練班、
　法界佛教大學、培德中學、育良小學等機構。

‧本會道場、機構,門戶開放,凡各國各教人士,
　願致力於仁義道德、明心見性者,歡迎前來共同研習!

DRBA

An Introduction to the Dharma Realm Buddhist Association

- Founder: Venerable Master Hsuan Hua
- Taking the Dharma Realm as its substance, DRBA seeks to disseminate the true principles of Buddhism to all areas of the world. Its missions are to translate the Buddhist scriptures, to propagate the orthodox Dharma, to promote ethics-based education, and to benefit all sentient beings.

- The guiding principles of **DRBA** are: no contention, no greed, no seeking, no selfishness, no seeking of personal advantage, and no lying.
- In addition to the City of Ten Thousand Buddhas, **DRBA** has nearly thirty branch monasteries located throughout the United States, Canada and Asia. **DRBA'S** Sangha members honor the rules and practices established by the Buddha: eating only one meal a day, always wearing the precept sash, observing the precepts and being mindful of the Buddha, studying the Buddha's teachings, practicing meditation, living together in harmony, and dedicating their lives to Buddhism.
- **DRBA'S** institutions include the International Institute for the Translation of Buddhist Texts, the Institute for World Religions, the Sangha and Laity Training Programs, Dharma Realm Buddhist University, Developing Virtue Secondary School, and Instilling Goodness Elementary School.
- The doors of **DRBA**'s monasteries and institutions are open to anyone from any country who wishes to devote themselves to the pursuit of humaneness, justice, and ethics, and the discovery of their true mind.

願將我應享受一切福樂

A Brief Introduction to the Venerable Master Hsuan Hua

宣化上人

簡傳

悉皆迴向普施法界眾生

I vow to fully take upon myself all sufferings
and hardships of all the living beings
in the Dharma Realm.

願將法界所有一切苦難
悉皆與我一人代受

來自白雪皚皚的中國東北長白山區。

十九歲出家修道，發願普度一切眾生。

一九六二年將正確真實的佛法，

由東方帶到西方——美國。

一九六八年五位美國人在上人座下出家，

是在西方建立三寶的第一人。

「美國法界佛教總會」創辦人，

分支道場遍佈美、加、亞地區。

建立美國第一座佛教大道場——萬佛聖城。

一九九五年圓寂，

「我從虛空來，回到虛空去」。

終其一生儘量幫助世界走向安樂光明的途徑，

大慈悲普渡，流血汗，不休息！

A Brief Introduction to the Venerable Master Hsuan Hua

He came from the snow-laden country
near the Eternally White Mountains in northeastern China.
At the age of nineteen,
he became a Buddhist monk and vowed to save all living beings.
In 1962, he brought the Proper Buddhadharma
from East to West (i.e., the U.S.).
In 1968, five Americans took monastic vows under his guidance.
Thus, he was the first person to establish the Triple Jewel
on American soil.
He founded the Dharma Realm Buddhist Association,
with branch monasteries in the United States, Canada,
Asia and Australia.
He established the City of Ten Thousand Buddhas,
the first large Buddhist monastic community in America

In 1995, before he passed into stillness, he said,
"I came from empty space, and to empty space I will return."
Throughout his life, through his own sweat and blood,
he helped the world walk towards the path of peace and light,
compassionately and tirelessly rescuing living beings.

May every living being,
Our minds as one and radiant with bright.
Share the fruits of peace,
With hearts of goodness,
luminous and bright.

願一切眾生心光朗耀，
以仁慈光明之心，
同享和平的果實。

法界佛教總會 · 萬佛聖城
Dharma Realm Buddhist Association &
The City of Ten Thousand Buddhas
4951 Bodhi Way, Ukiah, CA 95482 USA
Tel: (707) 462-0939   Fax: (707) 462-0949
http://www.drba.org , www.drbachinese.org

國際譯經學院 **The International Translation Institute**
1777 Murchison Drive, Burlingame, CA 94010-4504 U.S.A.
Tel: (650) 692-5912   Fax: (650) 692-5056

法界宗教研究院（柏克萊寺）
Institute for World Religions(at Berkeley Buddhist Monastery)
2304 McKinley Avenue, Berkeley, CA 94703 U.S.A.
Tel: (510) 848-3440   Fax: (510) 548-4551

金山聖寺 **Gold Mountain Monastery**
800 Sacramento Street, San Francisco, CA 94108 U.S.A.
Tel: (415) 421-6117   Fax: (415) 788-6001

金聖寺 **Gold Sage Monastery**
11455 Clayton Road, San Jose, CA 95127 U.S.A.
Tel: (408) 923-7243   Fax: (408) 923-1064

法界聖城 **City of the Dharma Realm**
1029 West Capitol Avenue, West Sacramento, CA 95691 U.S.A.
Tel/Fax: (916) 374-8268

金輪聖寺 **Gold Wheel Monastery**
235 North Avenue 58, Los Angeles, CA 90042 U.S.A.
Tel/Fax: (323) 258-6668

長堤聖寺 **Long Beach Monastery**
3361 East Ocean Boulevard, Long Beach, CA 90803 U.S.A.
Tel/Fax: (562) 438-8902

華嚴精舍 **Avatamsaka Hermitage**
11721 Beall Mountain Road, Potomac, MD 20854-1128 U.S.A.
Tel/Fax: (301) 299-3693

金峰聖寺 **Gold Summit Monastery**
233 First Avenue West, Seattle, WA 98119 U.S.A.
Tel: (206) 284-6690   Fax: (206) 284-6918

金佛聖寺 Gold Buddha Monastery
248 E. 11th Avenue, Vancouver, B.C. V5T 2C3 Canada
Tel: (604) 709-0248   Fax: (604) 684-3754

華嚴聖寺 Avatamsaka Monastery
1009 Fourth Avenue S.W., Calgary, AB T2P 0K8 Canada
Tel/Fax: (403) 234-0644

金岸法界 Gold Coast Dharma Realm
106 Bonogin Road, Mudgeeraba, QLD. 4213 Australia
Tel: (07) 5522-8788; 5520-1188

法界佛教印經會 Dharma Realm Buddhist Books Distribution Society
臺灣省臺北市忠孝東路六段 85 號 11 樓
Tel: (02) 2786-3022, 2786-2474   Fax: (02) 2786-2674

法界聖寺 Dharma Realm Monastery
臺灣省高雄縣六龜鄉興龍村東溪山莊 20 號
Tel: (07) 689-3713   Fax: (07) 689-3870

彌陀聖寺 Amitabha Monastery
臺灣省花蓮縣壽豐鄉池南村四健會 7 號 Tel: (03) 865-1956 Fax: (03) 865-3426

佛教講堂 Buddhist Lecture Hall
香港跑馬地黃泥涌道 31 號 11 樓
31 Wong Nei Chong Road, Top Floor, Happy Valley, Hong Kong, China
Tel: 2572-7644   Fax: 2572-2850

般若觀音聖寺 (紫雲洞)
Prajna Guan Yin Sagely Monastery (Formerly Tze Yun Tung Temple)
Batu 5 1/2, Jalan Sungai Besi, Salak Selatan,
57100 Kuala Lumpur, West Malaysia   Tel: (03)7982-6560 Fax: (03)7980-1272

法界觀音聖寺 (登彼岸)
Dharma Realm Guanyin Sagely Monastery (Formerly Deng Bi An Temple)
161, Jalan Ampang, 50450 Kuala Lumpur, Malaysia
Tel: (03) 2164-8055 Fax: (03) 2163-7118

馬來西亞法界佛教總會檳城分會
Malaysia Dharma Realm Buddhist Association Penang Branch
32-32C, Jalan Tan Sri Teh Ewe Lim,
11600 Jelutong,Penang, Malaysia
Tel: (04)281-7728 Fax: (04)281-7798

朝露

DEW DROPS

作　者　宣化上人
插畫者　王崇華

發行人　法界佛教總會
出　版　法界佛教總會・佛經翻譯委員會・法界佛教大學
　　　　The City of Ten Thousand Buddhas(萬佛聖城)
地　址　4951 Bodhi Way, Ukiah, CA 95482 USA
　　　　Tel: (707) 462-0939　Fax: (707)462-0949
　　　　http://www.drba.org , www.drbachinese.org

　　　　The International Translation Institute
　　　　1777 Murchison Drive Burlingame,
　　　　CA 94010-4504 U.S.A.
　　　　Tel: (650) 692-5912　Fax: (650) 692-5056

倡　印　萬佛聖城　The City of Ten Thousand Buddhas
　　　　4951 Bodhi Way, Ukiah, CA 95482 USA
　　　　Tel: (707) 462-0939　Fax: (707)462-0949

　　　　法界佛教印經會
　　　　Dharma Realm Buddhist Books Distribution Society
　　　　臺灣省臺北市忠孝東路六段 85 號 11 樓
　　　　11th Floor, 85 Chung-hsiao E. Road, Sec. 6,
　　　　Taipei, Taiwan, R.O.C.
　　　　電話: (02) 2786-3022, 2786-2474
　　　　www.drbataipei.org

出版日　2007 年 1 月 26 日・初版一刷
ISBN 978-088139-862-5